A Path to Peak Performance

Rob Cain

© 2012 Rob Cain
All Rights Reserved.

No part of this publication may be reproduced, stored in a retrieval system, or transmitted, in any form or by any means, electronic, mechanical, photocopying, recording, or otherwise, without the written permission of the author.

First published by Dog Ear Publishing
4010 W. 86th Street, Ste H
Indianapolis, IN 46268
www.dogearpublishing.net

ISBN: 978-1-4575-1536-1

This book is printed on acid-free paper.

Printed in the United States of America

Table of contents

Chapter 1 Getting Cash Under Control 5

Chapter 2 Authoring the Blueprint 12

Chapter 3 Product Rationalization—
Doing "Less" with Higher Standards 16

Chapter 4 Product Roadmap and
"Right-Sizing" the Business 23

Chapter 5 Instill a Culture of Execution
and Accountability 29

Chapter 6 People: The Key Ingredient 38

Chapter 7 Accelerating Top Line Growth
at Lower Costs 53

Chapter 8 Strategic Planning Process 57

Introduction

The purpose of this book is to guide the reader through the fundamental steps of improving company performance. Your business may be public, private, small cap, medium cap, in a distressed state, or performing well, but simply looking for an edge in your journey toward best-in-class or peak performance. In any case, the tools in this book are the fundamental elements to regularly increasing shareholder value predictably against plan. Although each business is different and each situation comes with its own timeline and complexities, I have found that the tools in this book are the fundamental ingredients to stabilize and increase the value of a company over time.

The tool kit I outlined in this book was developed by studying some of the best leaders of our time and combining this knowledge with my experience. The tools offer a simple method of identifying what is holding back your performance in a particular area, how to get your arms around it, and how to resolve it.

The one common theme you will find throughout this book is instilling a culture of accountability and execution, focus, and setting standards of excellence in everything we set out to accomplish. You will not find any fads or shortcuts here. Instead you will find simple tools ready to use and they all demand good old-fashioned hard work and the discipline to integrate them into your daily work routines.

Whether your company is a turnaround project or you just want to accelerate performance improvement, running the business to the proper set of assumptions and focus is essential. In its simplest form, the success of a project is largely based upon what assumptions we operate the business on and how quickly we integrate them into the business. The intention of this book is to act as a coach in challenging the current assumptions that are used to operate the business and to ensure they are the correct ones. Like stepping stones in our journey this book will suggest how to immediately validate (or change) your assumptions around cash, people, products, go-to market strategies, and more.

Planning and executing the project of improving company performance requires the right leader. This leader must be able to operate in a chaotic environment while simultaneously building and implementing an improvement plan that will remodel every part of the business. A seasoned turnaround leader is a vital ingredient to the success of the project, as he will have a knack for blending the decisions of daily chaos with the broader strategic issues and will be quick to spot issues with cash management, product performance, people, and more.

Reviving and remodeling distressed companies is one of my life's passions. I have been a part of some amazing teams of people with whom I'm proud to say I had an opportunity to work, but it's the failure that I was involved in that changed my life and ignited a fire within me. In short, I was part of an exciting OEM provider in the capital equipment space. Our team grew four times in both the top and bottom line, only to later be sold as a spare parts provider to the lowest-valued competitor in our field. Our team did many things right and had the heart of a champion, but the two mistakes we made changed the future of the business. I'll cover our mistakes and how to avoid them in chapters three and four.

As a result, I made a commitment to myself to never go through a failure again. I studied everything I could find about leadership and the drivers of success and failures from the experts of our time. I became trained in Six Sigma practices, the behavioral patterns of people, and how to lead in distressed times. Over the last twenty five years I have refined these tools and practices into a methodology to drive peak performance in people and companies. These tools are all part of the ***smart business system methodology***.

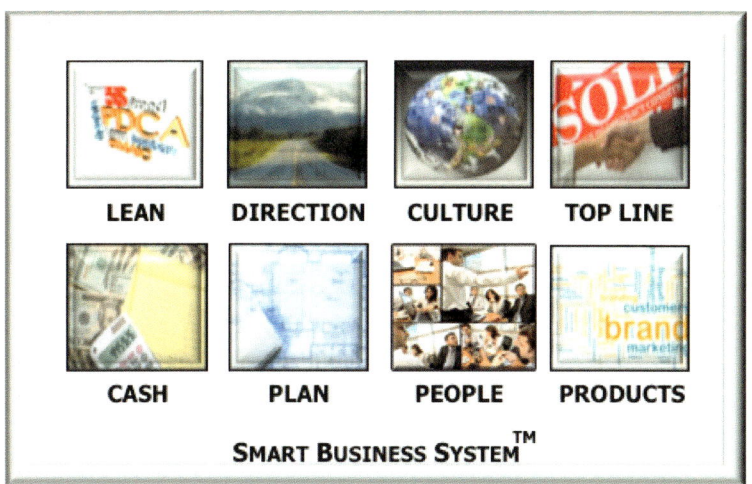

Each module of the *smart business system* impacts every part of the business, from financials to core competencies, markets, products, focus, and, of course, people.

I believe you will find this toolkit clearly outlined and easy to use. If you would like additional information or a free consultation on your project, please visit www.robcainconsulting.com.

I hope this book provides a framework for your company to become financially successful and to provide meaningful, fulfilling careers within the communities that your company impacts.

CHAPTER 1

Getting Cash Under Control

Chapter deliverables:

1. Getting cash under control
2. Daily cash practices
3. Building a new financial model
4. First impressions of the team

Getting cash under control

The lifeblood of any business is cash. Every business is in existence to generate cash and, ultimately, provide a predictable return to its shareholders. It's okay to say it over and over again, even in front of your customers: *We are in business to generate cash. Everything else we do is a means to that end.* It's the tip of the iceberg when setting the tone for the new culture, which will be described later in this book.

Most incumbent management teams believe they understand their financials, gross margins, and expenses. With distressed companies, I have yet to see this be true. With companies that are performing well, it can vary. It's not unusual to find that products that were thought to be generating cash were actually losing money. Facilities that were thought to be at full capacity actually had ample capacity for future new products and market demand.

A business must generate cash everything is a means to that end

There is almost always a material savings to be found within the fixed and variable costs of the business. Scouring every dollar spent and challenging ourselves to ensure it's the best value on the planet (if, in fact, we need to spend the money at all) is always an ingredient in getting full control of cash.

Incumbent management teams normally become comfortable with a particular product or factory making money. A fresh set of eyes and a different analysis may yield an entirely different result. Job number one is to emphatically understand cash. Understanding what truly generates cash and what is losing cash is the first job, with no exceptions. I highly recommend building a brand new model; often, when studying the current financial plan, which may not be leading the company to peak performance, it is harder to flush out those issues and assumptions that are sometimes outdated and flawed in a fast-paced marketplace.

Your first days on the project should be spent with the appropriate people in order to intimately understand the financials from every angle. These appropriate people range from the entire finance team to the shipping clerk. Taking one order and following it all the way through the company, from sales to payment and warranty, is a fast way to learn what really happens. Classic tools such as the income statement, balance sheet, and cash flow are only a simple warm-up in preparation for the work that lies ahead. A deeper analysis (and reality check for the tools in place) will show that it is best to start fresh and build a new model for every product and service offered. Validate direct and indirect costs as well as fixed and variable margins. Allocate all fixed costs and personnel to applicable products/services as appropriate and begin noticing the gaps between the tenured tools in place and the new tools.

Daily cash practices

Once a clear picture of cash is understood with certainty, it's time to take action as appropriate to stop the bleeding. There are seven traditional actions, which are listed here. Your team may choose one or all of them. If this is a new investment, I would strongly recommend you implement all of them, as implementing all of them will help you immediately learn more about the business and engage the whole team, allowing you to observe as part of the top grading process that is discussed later in this book.

Note: Even if your team has done these items before, if it's been a while, it's time to re-instill them in your culture. Some organizations that are performing well can slack off from these basic disciplines; plus, its fun to save money and run the company more competitively!

1. *Take control of the checkbook and sign every check.* You need to understand where every dollar is going and if the item/service the money is being spent on is the best value the team can find.

    a. Assign an owner to every expense item and hold that person accountable to ensure that expense is a business-critical expense and is, in fact, needed to operate the business. If so, coach this person to find the best value for the item.

    b. It is worthy of mention that reviewing checks is reactive, as the bill is now due and the damage is done. However, it does apply ownership to every dollar and is one of the fastest ways to understand how the company is currently spending cash. We will discuss later in this text why reactive leadership is poor leadership. It's likely that your distressed company does not have owners assigned to each expense item and has not instilled a process to regularly review expense items to ensure it is receiving the highest value people can find. This approach, while almost always needed, is simply plugging leaks in a dam. It is necessary, however, as it establishes the early stages of accountability.

  c. Be sure to do this your first day on the job. It provides an opportunity to read the impressions on people's faces as you hold them accountable down to the dollar level. These are great insights as we begin to top grade the team, which we will discuss later in this book.

2. *Establish a cash metric and a cash team.* Identify ONE cash owner. It will most likely be the CFO or yourself. This team will most likely meet daily or weekly to review cash and take necessary actions to meet bank covenants and board of director (BoD)-sanctioned plans. I typically put a policy in place of allowing only "business-critical" expenses. "Business critical" can mean a lot of things to different companies. A classic example of business-critical expenses is paying obligations such as payroll, suppliers, commissions, and financial notes. If it's not business-critical, it doesn't get spent. Guide the team through the process of defining what business-critical is.

3. *Establish a cross-functional team to find ways to reduce or even eliminate expenses.* Low-hanging fruit that can be eliminated typically includes such things as long-term facility leases, BoD fees, healthcare costs, and over-inflated/outdated insurance policies. Every bill needs to be reviewed with the goal of a better outcome. Assigning every line item on the income statement is always an eye opener.

4. *Schedule a Cash staff meeting.* Assign owners to every line item and tell these owners that all expenses start with $0 and need an ROI along with a purchase order before they will be approved. Some items are business-critical and should be pre-identified as such in order to circumvent the ROI process for these items.

5. *Approve all new business to ensure it is within the company's core competencies and meet gross margin and profit criteria, which we will discuss in the market and product section of this text.* Some incumbent management teams work to an outdated culture or set of rules that may allow non-profitable business in the door. Stop this before it begins: Endorse all new business and hold the Sales and Operations leaders accountable for meeting their numbers, resulting in the committed gross margin.

6. *Review bonus programs and ensure bonuses are based upon "new money" that is generated as a result of business profitability and growth.* If cash is not met, cancel all bonuses. It's the job of the leadership team to continually grow cash. If the team is not doing that, it is slowly suffocating the business and clearly its members do not deserve a reward for this level of performance.

Award bonuses based upon new money

7. *Approve any/all changes in compensation, including new hires, increases, changes in commission, and bonuses.*

Building a new financial model

For your company to exist, you must understand every dollar it spends and every dollar it generates. It must be right-sized between those two numbers in order to generate a profit and survive. It's that simple.

I have yet to see a leadership team of a distressed company understand their cash or their exact cost of goods sold or cash flow. Understanding how every dollar is allocated in the business is vital to making decisions with confidence. Take the time upfront, regardless of how painful it is, to truly understand cash: for example, the cost to win an order, the landed cost of a product, factory overhead rates, fixed and variable costs, the allocation of people to a product/service, product cost of ownership, and the cost of services offered. Once these costs are understood, decisions become very clear and you now have a baseline in which to begin crafting a turnaround plan.

During the process of getting cash under control, it will become clear whether or not the business has the fundamental building blocks to return the business to financial stability. As the turnaround leader, you need to validate quickly whether or not the business is salvageable and if it should be run for cash and immediately downsized with its current assets sold to repay obligations. Most distressed companies wait too long before sanctioning a turnaround program, making the odds of success lower the longer management delays. It's hard to announce that the company is distressed, and it's even harder to renovate the company into a mode where it can survive at a profitable level and be poised for growth. As the turnaround leader, your job is to quickly ascertain the available runway of the business in its current state and the options available to renovate and revive the business and to ultimately place it on a path of best-in-class shareholder value.

Phase I is about quickly identifying the health of the company with the help of detailed financial tools and proactive management of cash practices. The takeaways from this phase include product and service profitability, a culture of ensuring every dollar is the best value the company can find, and linking the reward systems to new money. Once this is achieved, phase II of the project can commence. Phase II focuses on aggressively growing the business and yielding best-in-class performance levels.

CHAPTER 2

Authoring the Blueprint

Chapter deliverables:

1. Defining "done"

2. A framework of the plan, including "Key Value Drivers"

3. Discussion with the owner/stakeholder(s)

Defining "done"

With basic financial tools now in place to monitor and control cash, it's time to author the turnaround plan. Each plan is different, and each depends on the available cash, timetable, and desired set of objectives. This chapter sets the framework of the turnaround plan. Each succeeding chapter then articulates each area of the plan.

It is critical that the turnaround/improvement plan contains all topics found in this book. Choosing to ignore any one of them will result in a Band-Aid approach and short-term gains at best.

There are generally six keys to a successful turnaround or performance improvement plan:

1. Define "done," being sure to be clear about when each interval of the turnaround/project will be complete

2. Have a main plan and contingency plans for each key objective

3. Assign one owner to the turnaround plan

4. Sanction the plan with the BoD and stakeholders

5. Measure the plan regularly and report data-driven performance

6. Place the plan under change control, requiring a formal session to change directions. Know that the plan will change several times, as turnarounds/improvement projects are never a straight line

Align with your customer and define done before you start

Authoring the definition of "done" is vital to any project, especially one as complex as a turnaround or improvement project. I learned about the "definition of 'done'" tool from Intel Corporation; it's a simple game changer that we use on all my projects. By requiring your customer to agree to a definition of "done," you are not only establishing the finishing line for the project, you are also discussing at length with the customer the many alternative solutions that exist to reach the desired state. The definition of "done" becomes the cover page to your plan and regular progress report, never allowing your audience to lose sight of the goal, as times will get hard and improvement projects are never a straight line. The following is an example of a project definition of "done":

1. 3X EBITDA in 3 years

2. Cash flow positive in under 12 months

3. Leadership team A players, all C players removed

4. Rationalize products, factories, and support infrastructure

5. 75% reduction of inventory

6. Best-in-class performance in NWC, inventory, lead time, product GM, COO, and MTBI

Authoring the definition of "done" is one of the exciting parts of the project for me, as it begins to illustrate the potential of the company and the many potential paths to reach the company's set of objectives. In a relatively short time the measuring points for your project will be obvious, as most of them are common metrics used within your particular space. Before sharing the framework of the success criteria with your customer, remind yourself that no part of an improvement project is ever a straight line. There are always several solutions for each known problem or desired outcome. In addition, there are always unforeseen problems throughout the business that can and will impact the best-laid plans.

A Framework for the turnaround plan including key value drivers

Each strategic action is labeled a "Key Value Driver." Simply stated, a Key Value Driver is a project that will materially change the value of the business. Typical examples include right-sizing the business by removing nonperforming products and people from the business, removing all noncore business and related costs from the company, establishing a regular stream of new revenue through new products/services, merger, acquisition, and refinancing. These are the high-profile projects that on their own also have an owner, a customer, and a definition of done and are tracked weekly for progress.

A path to peak performance is never a straightline; have contingency plans

As you build your action-tracking database, make it clear that there is one prime path to reach the objective and that there are alternative paths, or contingency plans. Most turnaround projects take at least a year. A lot of things can happen in the market within a year. Make it clear to your customer that this plan WILL change and alternative solutions are being thought through in the event they are needed.

I typically build an action-tracking database in which each tab is a critical element of the project and includes weekly agendas, a project cost/schedule, open/closed issues, and a decision log. An example of this tool can be found at www.robcainconsulting.com.

Discussion with shareholders

Identify the many stakeholders in the project. Stakeholders include the BoD, owner(s), shareholders, partners, suppliers, and, most vitally, the employees. They all play a role in the success of the project. As the coming chapters suggest, a number of ways to improve the business work through the communications for a set of stakeholders. I've found that when communicating the plan, communicating why the results of the plan are important is just as important as communicating about the project itself. Having canned "elevator" pitches ready for anticipated questions goes a long way in speeding the pace of the project and building the credibility of the team and yourself.

CHAPTER 3

Product Rationalization—Doing "Less" with Higher Standards

Chapter deliverables:

1. Understanding the current products' value-add

2. Voice of the customer

3. Answers to ten market-driven questions

4. Voice of the associate

5. Categorizing products into "Invest" "Sunset" or "End of Life"

Understanding the current products value-add

It's time for the next phase of heavy lifting, which is understanding the current product and service offering from a financial perspective and a marketplace perspective. The company's end game is to "do less, but with standards of excellence" and ensure that every offering is in fact generating cash. Most distressed companies chase revenue; management has the "bright, shiny object" syndrome and becomes distracted. That must be resolved, and it starts by narrowing down the company's offerings and identifying which products or services it plans to continue with or invest in; which products it plans to "sunset," or run for cash; and which products it plans to "end of life." Once this set of decisions is made, our next step is to develop a product and service roadmap that will set the pace for the business in generating new revenue streams annually.

The first task is to understand the competitive advantage of the company's products and services from a market perspective. This work may be completed with some internal support, but must be validated with outside experts, including key customers, from a number of angles. Most distressed companies have become "inside-out" in their thinking and have not led the market. Inside-out thinking means that they think of ideas internally and then take that idea to market, "hoping" their solution is competitive and generates revenue.

Establish a "outside – in" process and regularly gain the voice of the customer

Conversely, prime organizations are "outside-in" thinking and listen intently to the market before developing a regular stream of new products that answer the call of tomorrow and beyond. "Outside-in" thinking teams develop a new product and feature roadmap and are constantly looking for an advantage via intellectual property or unique applications. Their goal is to develop a product that can only be purchased from their company. Although these situations are rare, when they do happen, they can change the game for years while competitors struggle to catch up.

Voice of the customer

There is nothing more valuable than the voice of the customer, particularly when that customer is offering constructive criticism. In addition, you may want to consider meeting with industry experts, hearing their data-driven opinions, and then factor them into your thinking. One of the objectives of gathering this data is to validate whether or not the suite of products and services is a commodity, a product that can be purchased from many different companies or a "value add," a product that can only be purchased from a specific business, in the eyes of your customers. If the suite of products is thought of as a commodity, is there a path to improve or alter the products that would change them to a value add and ultimately provide a material advantage in the market?

If the family of products will remain a commodity, the next step becomes all the more important. This next step is identifying your smoking gun and the reason that customers buy from you instead of your competitors. As discussed previously, this should be the result of talking with several customers that provide open, honest, constructive criticism.

The takeaways from field due diligence include such questions as, "Why do customers buy from us," "Why do we lose sales," and "What improvements can we make to close more sales in a shorter cycle time and with less effort?"

Voice of the associates

The next set of interviews to answer these and other questions should include your associates and key suppliers, if appropriate. *"Associates know the real problems of the organization and products and are waiting for management to do something about it"* (Colin Powell). Make time to speak with the people selling, designing, building, shipping, and servicing the products in question. They know the problems associated with the products, and many are well in tune with their competitors' strengths and weaknesses.

Two of the tools I commonly use to help guide this process are a two-by-two matrix and the company's core competencies. A two-by-two matrix can be helpful to capture a great deal of information, to communicate the current landscape, and to follow an action plan. Core competencies describe both what the organization does and what it does not do, and it is a powerful document to use to shift a culture quickly. The following graphic is an example of a two-by-two matrix that communicates the landscape of a past project.

Existing Products	New Products
Current Opportunities ■ Expand into adjacent markets *Future Opportunities* New Product Application Acquisition / Merger	*Future Opportunities* New market strategy IP strategy
Current Opportunities ■ Proactive business in emerging countries ■ Product application; capacity / cycle time / CoO *Future Opportunities* New material applications Deeper business with existing customers	*Current Opportunities* ■ New material application with IP ■ Value chain integration *Future Opportunities* Global service business including competitor roll up Acquisition: Product line extensions

Getting answers to ten market driven questions

Before jumping to any conclusions based upon market Intel, you should mentally challenge the performance potential of the current products and the current team. You will need answers to the following questions prior to making any final decisions:

1. What is the available market? Is it served with commodity or value add products? Is the market growing or shrinking?

2. What are the predicted inflexion points, or game changers, in the market? How will the existing products perform before, during, and after the inflexion points have taken place?

3. Are today's products commodities or value add in the customer's mind? (Commodities always mean lower GM and a dogfight to win the business.)

4. What work is needed to turn our commodity products into value add products?

   i. Re-engineering- improving the design of the product to operate more efficiently at a lower costs for example

   ii. Integrate intellectual property – Improving the design to incorporate intellectual property and thereby provide a unique solution in the market.

   iii. Integrate two or more commodities into one custom product solution. Combine two products into one possibly reducing the overall size, cost of two products and reducing the number of steps in a manufacturing process for the customer.

   iv. Add services to the product offering – possibly integrate a service model into the OEM product by combining price of the product with an annual service program.

5. What effort would need to be made in order to increase the close rate?

6. What part of our go-to market strategy is not working: marketing channels, sales execution, product performance, or all three?

7. Can we sell existing solutions into adjacent, up, or down markets to meet revenue and GM objectives?

8. How do we compare to best-in-class close rates? Are we product selling or education-based selling?

9. Are we fully exploiting the spares and service business of our OEM offering?

10. Is there an opportunity for merger or intellectual property acquisition from this field or another to change the game?

Categorizing products into "Invest" " Sunset" or "End of Life"

With our latest market Intel in hand, it's now appropriate to determine the future of every product and service by placing each product or service into one of three categories: invest, sunset, and end of life. "Invest" means that the product has a strong future; it has both a best-in-class GM and performance in the market. It may or may not be a commodity. If it is a commodity, a thorough analysis should be undertaken in order to understand what options are available to reposition the product as value add in the customers' eyes. One classic option is a product redesign incorporating intellectual property.

"Sunset" means that this product is at the end of its life and is clearly a commodity. A product is "sunset" instead of "end of life" when its current margins are helping the business increase the combined margin of all products and it is still needed to run for cash, as this will be a major contributor in funding the product roadmap. Finally, "sunset" means that this product may be around for some time, but that the company will not apply forward-looking resources to this product. Simply said, the company will collect revenue from existing customers with this product and terminate any engineering efforts. In the coming months, the business will work to gracefully transition these customers to longer-term products.

"End of life" occurs when the product will no longer be offered and is removed from all sales and marketing literature. The company will not expend any additional effort on the product other, and it will transition the install base to a more competitive solution if one is offered.

The company needs three pieces of information: (a) market Intel, (b) answers to the tenquestions introduced previously in the chapter, and (c) updated financial model before it can reach its end objective of "doing less, but with standards of excellence." (Remember that most distressed companies have entirely too much on their plates, have an unclear direction, and are only doing average work on everything.) The company should strive to have three products long-term, but in the near term, some products may be placed in a "sunset" category, which may require resource allocation for a year or more.

CHAPTER 4

Product Roadmap and "Right-Sizing" the Business

Chapter deliverables:

1. New product roadmap

2. Establishing a new stream of revenue

3. Right-sizing the business

4. Rationalization plan

New Product Roadmap

With the current product family categorized into one of three categories (invest, sunset, or end of life), it's time to build the product roadmap. The end game here is to quickly increase gross margins and add profitable market share by fundamentally solving the customer's current problems. The company's new products come with a "price of entry," or elements they must have in order to make our roadmap. Some of the most common "price of entry" points are best-in-class gross margin, cost of ownership and whether or not they are value-add, meaning that the solution can only be purchased from this company. Our work in this phase of the turnaround focuses on establishing inflexion points of higher margins, growing market share, and setting the pace for the business by unveiling regular streams of new revenue.

Commodity products all provide relatively the same performance, lifetime, and price. Providing a commodity product means that deals are won on price and lead time. To the provider, this means definitely shrinking margins and adding to current inventory to reduce cycle times, both being evils in the world of lean enterprise. To the consumer, this is great news: bidding wars become the norm in these instances. Your job as the turnaround agent is to avoid these battles by providing longer-term, value-add solutions.

In contrast, a value add product either introduces a new solution to the market or consolidates a number of existing solutions into a new offering, saving the customer cycle time, space, and operating costs. Value add products eventually become commodities. Recognizing that and proactively building a roadmap that integrates intellectual property into the product is the first step to getting in front of competitors.

We typically set four goals when developing a product roadmap:

1. Develop a family of value add products meeting the previously mentioned "price of entry" requirements

2. Set the expectation and pace of new product rollouts

3. Provide a platform for strategic thinking

4. Execute to committed product cost and project schedule.

Selecting the team to build the roadmap is a critical decision that should be given considerable time and thought. Clearly, the roadmap needs an owner, and that should be a CTO or chief scientist if that person has the needed skill set, which will be defined later in this book. The rest of the internal team should be made up of a senior engineer, the sales leader, and the marketing leader. If you have not already significantly changed up the leadership team, it's probably wise to bring in some outside thinking to aggressively challenge this group. In past projects, I have established "technical advisory groups" that include the team suggested as well as outside marketing experts, key customers, and even technical board members.

Provide the team members with homework prior to their first meeting. Direct them to the new culture, which will be described later in this book, and describe the hard and soft skills that are required to be on this team. Have the owner of the roadmap send out a template of the roadmap and the deliverables expected of the first series of meetings.

Be sure to tell them that the document is under change control and should be supported by the forecast sales plan. Roadmaps are to be updated monthly and presented to the BoD quarterly, sharing progress and new thinking with them.

Depending on the culture and the maturity of the team, at this point I may choose to add a new layer to the company culture. Later in this book we will discuss that every culture is about accountability and execution. The company should not tolerate repeated mistakes or missed deadlines, as it will require its teams to be expert-level planners and executers In contrast we will often times encourage R&D Teams to take risk and "fail fast" as break through results require taking risk. New solutions are generally developed out of a series of failures to try something new. Therefore, failing fast in an R&D environment can sometimes produce long term value-add products. If your team has the maturity and has embraced the culture described later in this book, this is a perfect time to coach the R&D Team in how to fail fast. These practices are described at www.robcainconsulting.com.

In order for roadmaps to be complete, they must include the following components:

1. Trends in the market
2. Voice of the customer

3. New technology
4. Available IP (from this field and others)
5. SWOT analysis
6. Lessons learned
7. Performance report card
8. New product development process
9. Annual change up of the team

Establishing a Stream of New Revenue

With a version 1.0 roadmap in hand, it's now time to ask the roadmap team to build a new product development process. One of the team's goals is to regularly introduce a new value add product to the market. There are many best-in-class companies to benchmark from as you undertake this process. My advice is to review four or five models and then build one that works specifically in your field or company. Keep it simple and measureable. This process, and the roadmap, will be reviewed monthly for performance to plan and accountability.

The following graphic illustrates the classic stage gates contained in a new product development process. Your business may require slight modifications to this process, but, in general, all of these steps are required in order to have a proactive approach to both product management and solving customers' problems with well-thought out solutions. Like all key processes in the business, this process needs an owner and a set of KPIs (key performance indicators, or metrics) to measure progress and results. Typical KPIs include both new revenue generated from the process and elimination of the reasons that the company used to lose orders.

Classic New Product Development Process

Right-Sizing the Business

With the current products categorized and a product roadmap in place, it is now time to right-size the business based upon the suite of products and services it offers. The financial model built in chapter one will serve as the backbone to understanding the financial impact on the business. Our goal here is to right-size the business one time to avoid prolonged disruption throughout the business. This means people and support costs related to each product line are eliminated or reduced. Right-sizing a business is never easy, but the golden rules are to cut once and cut deeper than needed; Remove all average leaders when removing people (the workers know who these average leaders are and they have been waiting for you to do something about it); and to let the "A-player" employees, regardless of title, step up and run smaller or medium-sized teams. This process is about changing the face of the business quickly; it is another step in the culture shift that we will discuss later in this book.

The deliverables from this set of decisions include

1. Updated financial plan
2. Current and future suite of products and services
3. A new product development process
4. Right-sized business with lower fixed and variable costs
5. New leadership team
6. Monthly set of performance objectives

With these decisions and your backup data in hand, it's time to meet with your customer (and the BoD) to discuss the rationalization process, the recommendation for new products, and the details of right-sizing the business, including a new financial plan and a new team.

CHAPTER 5

Instill a Culture of Execution and Accountability

Chapter deliverables:

1. A culture of accountability and execution

2. Meetings and using your time more effectively than your competitors

3. Accountability tools

4. Speaking a language of accountability

A culture of accountability and execution

Two skills are vital in any business: the ability to make the **right** plan and the ability to execute that plan. Execution is a passion for me both personally and professionally. I've been a student of execution for thirty years, and I plan to be one for the next thirty.

I have never seen a distressed company with the right culture. Most are country club environments with few KPIs and very low accountability. This is mainly because the leadership team is not making good decisions, and they know it, so they forgive the workforce by not holding themselves or the business accountable.

Dozens of studies conclude that it takes seven to ten years to truly change the culture of a business. They may be right, but my experience has been that you can make lasting change in six months, though this change is painful. I've found the more painful you make it and the faster you force the change, the more successful it is. I don't say this to be mean or cold. Use the pain as your leverage to accelerate the change and make the new culture stick.

After a short time in the company I build the tools and processes it believes are correct for the business, and then crafts these tools and processes into a new-culture "course" that is mandatory for all employees. I typically teach the course myself, as I'm looking for early warning signs of who will honestly adopt the new culture and who is simply paying lip service.

In the course, I typically outline the direction of the company, then move on to an accountability tracking tool. From this moment forward, all company objectives have owners, commitment dates, and a definition of "done." I then share the schedule of planning meetings we will attend, including the point at which the owners of these key deliverables will have the time to work with their customers, internal or external, to define "done" and agree on the timetable. The new culture should NOT be dictatorial, but should be fiercely accountable.

Meetings and using our time more effectively than our competitors

In the next part of the course, I will outline how precious our time as a team is and what using time effectively looks like, including when we should meet and when we should not meet.

I typically ONLY suggest meeting for

1. Impact meetings
2. One-on-one meetings
3. Staff meetings
4. Performance evaluation meetings
5. Company meetings

All other meetings are to be cancelled. There has not been a distressed company that I have worked with yet in which I have not cancelled all meetings the executive team had, as they were not productive. This also provides a helpful shift to the new culture.

People in the company should only meet to solve problems or share information. The following points are some steps to an effective meeting.

1. Meetings should be scheduled ahead of time. Agendas, action-tracking documents, and decision logs that are managed by the owner or meeting host should be sent to meeting attendees in advance.

2. Homework should be sent out and assigned to owners ahead of time.

3. Meetings should start and end on time.

4. In the first 5 minutes, the meeting host should review the purpose of the meeting and the content of the agenda and ask if there are any changes. The host should expect none.

5. Meeting attendees should cover the content of the agenda and update the action-tracking documents and decision logs.

6. Meeting attendees should confirm the next meeting if needed.

The tools for accountability are nothing new. The team needs to enforce them with a fierce discipline and must be emphatic about assigning an owner and customer to every project and defining "done" before starting a project. Turnarounds have enough surprises on their own due the fast pace and the level of risk. In order to minimize surprises using the project planning tools described in this text and communication tools such as the

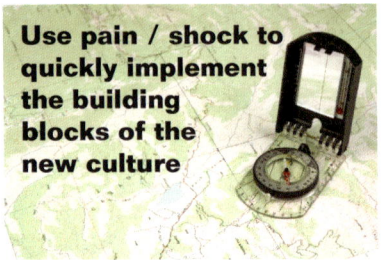

Use pain / shock to quickly implement the building blocks of the new culture

Indian talking stick from Stephen Covey will help keep the execution level as high as possible. The Indian talking stick is a technique to requires proactive listening to ensure the communication is being heard. This is a profound tool we use on all our projects. Once that is completed, the team must be fierce about, "doing what we said we would do."

Tools for accountability

1. Action-tracking database
2. Decision log
3. Key performance indicators
4. Company objectives, monthly deliverables
5. Board plan

Speaking the language of accountability

In a new culture, people speak a different language. They are taught new definitions for old words. Those not using the terms are probably not bought in to the culture shift. Speak with them again once they have completed the new-culture introduction course. If they are in a leadership role and do not make the shift, release them from the business. The new culture is the backbone of the turnaround; the company must have zero tolerance for late adopters at the leadership level.

Terms we speak:

1. **Definition of "done"**—Leadership hates surprises and will NOT start a project until the customer and supplier agree to what "done" means.

2. **Customer**—the one person that must earn revenue or improve the performance of the business when the problem is resolved.

3. **Owner**—the one person that is responsible to resolve the issue per the definition of "done." This person can make no excuses if the issue is not resolved in a timely manner.

4. **Action log**—a simple tool that tracks performance on a weekly basis. This tool also documents the definition of "done," cost, and schedule.

5. **Decision log**—a simple tool that tracks decisions made, the data used to make the decision, and who owns the decisions.

6. **Impact meeting**—A weekly performance meeting in which a cross-functional team meets to positively "impact" performance. Impact meetings are scheduled for every department in the company.

7. **One on one meeting**—A meeting between a direct-report employee and his supervisor to ensure he is doing what he said he would do and to discuss the six human needs.

8. **Six human needs**—Adopting Tony Robbins's work, where applicable, is helpful in turning around distressed companies, and following the six human needs has been a game changer. This is discussed in detail in chapter six.

9. **Commitment date**—a date agreed to by both an owner and a customer. It will be made, and no excuses will be accepted should it pass without the finished product.

10. **"Date for a date"**—when an owner cannot provide a commitment due to lack of information or planning, this owner is to provide a date on which he will know and be able to set a commitment date. This is a "date for a date."

11. **Top grading score card**—a score card that describes why a certain position exists in the company and details the performance required for anyone occupying that position. The below graphic provides a generic example of a top grading score card. For further information on the top grading process the text entitled Top Grading by Brad Smart along with his website is a terrific source of information. **Current state**—the current state of performance.

    Top grading score cards define the performance of a position and help speed accountability

12. **Future state**—the set of objectives and performance criteria that define where the team expects to be in the future.

13. **KPI**—Key Performance Indicator. It is a metric in which the company measures itself against the best-in-class. Each KPI has one owner; it also has an action plan to reach best-in-class if the company is not currently there.

14. **KVD**—Key Value Drivers. These are strategic objectives that will materially improve the value of the business. A key value driver typically requires board-level endorsement, an owner, customer, definition of "done," and is measured weekly.

Job Card				
Name		Name here		
Title		Chief Operating Officer		
Time in role		1 month		
Career level experience		20 years		
				Gaps to becoming an A
A,B,C Player		TBD		1. learn the industry
				2
				3
Growth / Development plan endorsed?		No		TBD
Why does this role exist				
1 lead us out of the go-go phase and into a prime performing organization				
2 Teach us how to plan and execute strategically and tactically				
3 Teach us accountability and how to aggressively grow our business strategically and tactically				
4 Help the CEO inspire the right team to standards of excellence				
Fundamental traits of the position		H, M, L		
Trait		Importance	Track record	Comments
Credible leader trusted by customers and associates		H	TBD - 3/1	
Inspires all around him		H	TBD - 3/1	
High Energy		H	TBD - 3/1	
Finds solutions / not excuses		H	TBD - 3/1	
Operates from the heart, but uses his head		H	TBD - 3/1	
Aggressive follow through		H	TBD - 3/1	
Makes time to be proactive		H	TBD - 3/1	
Confident street fighter		H	TBD - 3/1	
Runs to facts/data		H	TBD - 3/1	
Can disagree and commit		H	TBD - 3/1	
Raw intelligence with money and people		H	TBD - 3/1	
Persistent		H	TBD - 3/1	
Key accountabilities		H, M, L		
		Importance	Date	Comments
1 Implements company wide execution tools		H	1-Apr	Agendas, meeting plan Project plan, CO, a way of work
2 Coaches the implementation of NPD tools		H	1-May	NPD tools a way of work for Accessline
3 Instills accountability in every leader in the business		H	1-Apr	Action items logs tracking % of Execution target 85%
4 Coached the implementation of strategic roadmaps		H	15-Jun	TAG, Roadmap development and update a way of work
5 Implements leadership tools to grow team		H	1-Jun	Performance enhancement, leadership, team building
6 Reduces waste in the company, minimizing rework		H	15-Jun	Frees up 15% of our capacity

H, M Denotes High, Medium, Low

A few weeks after the course, make time to follow up with the workforce. Schedule roundtable sessions with three to six first-line employees in which you can Ask them if their management teams are using the tools they'd been taught and if they are seeing different results. Listen to their feedback and take it to heart. Most first-line employees know the problems the company is facing and are waiting for strong leadership to engage the right tools, terminate non-effective people, and provide clear direction and results.

A six-month culture shift comes with pain, and your job is to inflict the pain. Be sure to do it in such a way that the team feels it would result in more pain to stay in the old culture. It's easy to communicate to the team what would happen if they stayed on the current path. Those that want to stay on the current path need to be removed, and quickly. When this happens, call a staff meeting and make it known that not using the new tools is not acceptable. Prepare canned speeches explaining to the team why it's more painful to stay in the current state than it is to change and move to the future state. Cite examples of how good it will **feel** to move to the future state.

Finally, measure the culture implementation. This is subjective, *but if you can't measure it, it won't get done.* (One of the motto's of Jack Welch). One of my favorite KPIs for culture is companywide execution. I start measuring this the day I walk in the door. Most distressed company's execution percentage ranges between 50 and 60 percent. This means they complete about half of what they said they would complete. There is a long list of excuses, and they often sound like this:

We changed our plans…so I did not have to finish.

When I started doing this work…it was much bigger than I thought…I need another month.

We started, but we did not have the budget to finish.

In six months or less, the companywide execution needle typically moves to 80 percent. After a year, it typically levels out at the low/mid 90s. The reasons that this KPI goes up so radically in such a short period of time are many the following serve as a few of the typical reasons. The following are a few key reasons.

We learn to plan impeccably well.

We define what "done" means before we start a project.

Our project plans have an owner, a customer, a definition of "done," and a weekly measuring system that we review in our weekly impact meetings.

We take on fewer projects.

We preach "DWWSWWD" (Do What We Say We Will Do), which means to be careful of what you say, because we are going to hold you accountable.

We establish core competencies so that we know what we do as a company and what we do NOT do, thereby giving us license to say no, since we are now generating cash on the core products of the business.

We keep the R&D teams out of this cycle. We want them to fail, and fail fast. This will be discussed later in this text.

CHAPTER 6

People: The Key Ingredient

Chapter deliverables:

1. How to identify a C player (low performers)

2. Inspiring people to new levels of performance

3. Rewarding A players (top performers)

4. Tony Robbins's six human needs

5. Leading people during distressed times

How to identify a C player (low performers)

Your first day on the job, you began the most critical task of all: analyzing the talent pool and identifying the A-level, B-level, and C-level talent. You must ask yourself this question: Are the leaders capable of making decisions, saying no to the wrong ideas, planning and executing the right ideas, and holding the team accountable? I must admit that I start every project at a distressed company with the belief that the team that brought the business to the point of distress will never be the same team that turns the business back to a cash-flow positive state and on to greater shareholder value. Furthermore, if the company has been distressed for any amount of time, the A-level talent in the company has probably left. If you are lucky, you are left with a flawed executive team, a few B players, and a busload of C players.

The team that brought the company down will not be the same team that turns it around

These are harsh words and I realize that, but I have another belief: People are the most vital ingredient to improving the performance of a business or executing a turnaround. I have found that without the right people in the right positions, higher-level performance is not sustainable. This belief is exactly why I typically start each project with the previously discussed leadership new-culture course outlining the culture and the six human needs. These two items quickly illustrate which leaders are ready for higher-level performance and which ones will resist it.

A seasoned turnaround leader operates around two rules simultaneously: Rule number one is that everything must generate cash; everything else is a means to that end. Rule number two is to start with the people first. Get the right people on the bus and in the right seats; get the wrong people off the bus, and quickly.

One of the single most important jobs of a turnaround leader is to identify the current talent pool and design and execute a restructuring of the business around long term products and services and the resources needed to execute those products and services. Because we are dealing with people, some leaders become emotional. They have not been trained to manage with facts and data within a culture of accountability. When it comes to people, the rules are actually easy to identify and enforce. The following eight points help to identify leaders that are not performing well.

Leaders are C players and need to be separated if demonstrate any of the below listed behaviors:

1. They do not have a clear direction forward.

2. They do not have a clear set of monthly or quarterly objectives.

3. They do not hold themselves or their teams accountable.

4. They have run the business into a distressed state due to wrong assumptions.

5. They chase the next shiny object.

6. They are "inside-out" thinkers.

7. They are not inspiring leaders.

8. They become argumentative when discussing new ideas and practices such as accountability tools, new product-development practices, and top grading score cards.

Depending on the situation, it's best to do one major restructure quickly so the surviving team knows that is the only reorganization so long as everyone meets their performance goals and they can once again focus on the task at hand. Give yourself a few weeks on the job to find the C level within the senior management team and one level down from there. Then develop a plan to restructure the business ASAP and review it with the BoD and the business owner. This will not be a surprise if your definition of "done" clearly states that you will require A players at the C level and at senior levels.

Instead of starting executive searches to replace all the people you plan to remove and waiting until you find the right candidate, remove these people ASAP and require the first-line management to step up in acting roles. Make it clear that you are searching for long-term replacements and that they should formally apply for the position if they want to be included in the process in this new role.

Inspiring people to new levels of performance

Inspiring people to new levels of performance is a key part of every project. Each time teams posted incredible results like triple digit improvement in YOY EBITDA, these teams had trust, alignment of common goals, were using the tools and terms cited in the previous chapter, and were deeply integrated into the business. I regularly use tools from Tony Robbins and Steven Covey. In particular, I use the six human needs and the seven habits of highly effective people, respectively. By integrating this skill set into the culture, people quickly find a way to win; politics and excuses are abolished, as people within the company simply do not have time for them.

Every time the companies I have worked with have developed long-term shareholder value, the root of it was an inspired team that had the company's full trust and respect and had a deep passion to win. In order to get to that point, take the following steps:

1. Clearly describe the goals of the organization
2. Align the purpose of the company to those goals
3. Give the team ownership and support
4. Train people
5. Reward people
6. Deeply involve people in the business
7. Manage to the six human needs
8. Spend quality time as a way of work

Below is portion of a company direction we put in place during a past project. In this direction, we specifically describe our expectation of people and how we plan to invest in them. Each situation is different, though. Think through what is appropriate for your situation, communicate it, and then execute it. Remember, you have two jobs: Guide the development of the right plan and coach people in how to execute better than your competitors. I will also happily point out that some of the direction below was authored by a key technical leader on a past project. The point here is twofold: The first point is that leadership should bring out the best in people and showcase skills. The second point is to give credit where credit is due.

Example of company direction describing our focus on people

Every employee will be measured on alignment to our plan and execution within their area and special project teams. Employees will be expected to understand, challenge and support our journey to excellence. Clearly stated, accepting status quo will not be tolerated. Every employee will be given the tools and opportunity to improve on a regular basis and challenged to do so through proactive, engaging leadership practices.

We will invest heavily into our workforce. Investments will be focused through the fundamentals of leadership where we expect the outcome to be a workforce that plans and executes well to a predetermined plan. A workforce that is inspired, and challenges our plans and is devoted to the success of our customers and shareholders.

Our leadership team will be measured on inspiring their troops. Clearly articulating our purpose and setting standards of excellence in everything we do. Leaders will be expected to provide solutions to help them in becoming high performing groups that deeply understand their deliverables internally and externally with a no excuses management approach.

Parts of our business will be measured on taking calculated risks, while others will be measured on flawless execution. We coach existing talent to world class levels and provide regular training to ensure our team is properly armed to set standards of excellence in the market.

Our work force will be measured on "doing what we said we would" and is held accountable to our core KPI's meeting world class standards. Our dashboard will include metrics for Quality, Cost, Delivery and Morale throughout our business. Our leadership team will adopt techniques from the top well run businesses in our nation to continue to improve regularly. Our philosophy is the one of continual improvement and that starts with our leadership team and then our workforce.

Continually train the team. I generally have a four– to five-day leadership training course. I custom-build the course for each project, covering the weak parts of the current culture and clearly articulating the conditions of employment. The last day of class, every leader signs a contract that states they understand the "price of entry" to be a leader and that they will commit to our new way of work. This course is packed with interaction and small breakout groups so that I can watch people work and further challenge and improve my thinking on the top grading plan. The course is also intended as a tool to inspire people that want the company to turn around. It easily identifies people that are burned out and think the company owes them something for the pain they have endured over time, as well. I would highly recommend this approach, as I have found this an invaluable learning tool for the participants and myself.

After the initial leadership course, host monthly sessions. Depending upon your situation, you may want to focus on sacred cows and hidden agendas and ensure these are broken down quickly. Another approach during these monthly sessions is to role-play with the new-culture tools and allow the team a venue to practice this new way of work.

Rewarding A players (top talent)

Reward the remaining team well. Rewards come in many ways. The first should be involvement in making and executing the turnaround plan. The second should be compensation. Pay your A players competitively and establish pay-for-performance bonus programs that have significant upsides when objectives are met or even exceeded. If available, properly allocate stock options, grants, or other ownership vehicles in which the real reward occurs when the company wins and increases a stock price significantly. After all, this is the end game. Develop a reward program in which key employees are handsomely rewarded by growing shareholder value. This is a vital element in connecting people to the direction of the company and annually planning and maintaining priority.

There are numerous cost-free or nearly cost-free rewards, as well. Make time to catch people doing things right, as Ken Blanchard taught us, then select random rewards and ensure these people are rewarded when they demonstrate the new culture and do what they say they will do.

Rewards play a large role in demonstrating who the key people are and who is making the shift to the new culture and generating results. Make some rewards, such as a larger computer screen or a company jacket, visible. Do this in a positive way and you will notice others wanting to become recognized. Positive public recognition can be a large motivator. In monthly company meetings, the companies I consult with cover direction, financial performance, new products, market update, recognition, and Q&A.

Only spend your time with high performers. If you are meeting with a lower performer, it should be to discuss an action plan to increase performance levels or to separate the person from the business. People want to be with other winners. Reward high performers by prioritizing your time with them.

Tony Robbins six human needs

A deeper look at rewarding people and understanding people is taught to us by Tony Robbins through instructing us on the six human needs that everyone has. I have used these needs as the cornerstone of my personal and professional life, and it's been the single biggest game changer for me.

Tony Robbins teaches us that everyone, no matter what race, position, gender, or age we are, has the same needs. If those needs are being met, a person is very likely to be happy. If those needs are not being met, this person may well develop into a low-performing employee or an unhappy spouse/partner. The takeaway here is that you need to understand these needs and implement them into your culture at work and your personal life. It will change your life. The following graphic gives a high-level summary of the six human needs.

1. **Certainty**—Everyone wants some level of certainty in his life. Some want more than others. Certainty comes at all levels and brings calm to our life, while not enough certainty brings chaos and kills productivity. Too much certainty brings boredom and slows productivity. It's your job as a leader to find the balance in your team and your company. Examples of certainty are knowing an assignment won't change; knowing the house will still be there and family will be home when someone arrives home; and knowing that the company's products will perform to specification.

2. **Uncertainty**—Just as everyone needs some level of certainty in his life, everyone needs some level of

uncertainty. Uncertainty entails not knowing the exact route to turn a company around on day one, or surprising your spouse with a dream vacation or a weekend getaway. Uncertainty comes in many forms. It's your job as a leader to provide uncertainty in the organization and in career plans. If a person stays in a position too long, too much certainty can settle in and that part of the organization becomes stale. You can bring in uncertainty by launching programs such as "one new product a year" or eliminating inventory—not reducing it, but eliminating it—or executing a merger or acquisition.

3. **Significance**—Everyone needs to feel significant in her work and personal life. Significance can be seen by completing a project at work that is meaningful to the long-term growth of the company. You could lead a project to refinance the company, develop a new product, change the company name, or something like this. Your job as a leader is to ensure that employees have the appropriate level of significance by ensuring they are working on challenging projects that are directly linked to company success.

4. **Love/Connection**—Everyone wants love and connection both at home and at work. As a leader, you provide love and connection by inspiring people to the next level, properly rewarding them, and telling them you care about them professionally. In one-on-one sessions, be sure to regularly talk about love and connection of all key employees. Yes, you should use the word "love." A company should love its people and results; it loves to win. Winning occurs when a team of people plan and execute better than their competitors. Team members knowing they are part of a team that deeply cares for its employees raises standards of execution.

5. **Growth**—Everyone wants personal and professional growth. Growth drives uncertainty during the learning process and later drives certainty. For example, if you are learning to play the guitar, the first time you pick it up, you feel awkward and uncertain. As the lessons continue, the feeling of holding the guitar is more certain; gradually, a few chords inspire confidence. As a leader, your job is to ensure that your key leaders are growing using documented career plans and measured objectives that challenge their current skills so they are more valuable to the company in the coming year.

6. **Contribution**—Everyone needs contribution in his personal and professional life. Contribution is giving back to the company or the relationship. For example, a company may decide to break into an Asian market. An employee may be fluent in the local language and customs, and she can teach a series of courses to the company as a way of contributing to the company. This project would encompass certainty, uncertainty, significance, and growth, as well. In your personal life, if you are raising children, your contribution will be high as you teach your children how to be good people daily. With your partner/spouse, you may find your chance to contribute comes by providing stability and supporting his or her goals and dreams.

On all our projects each month we have one-on-one meetings to discuss the performance of employees and team members during the previous month and the expectations for the coming month. Part of this discussion is based on the six human needs. In some companies, we display the six human needs on the one-on-one meeting agenda and on white boards in all the offices and conference rooms. If the needs of our high performers are met, they will stay. If they are not met, they will leave. A critical element to increasing long-term shareholder value is executing the plan in a clear direction and managing to the six human needs.

COMPANY NAME HERE						
John Jackson, VP of Sales monthly 1:1 performance review						
Day						
Time						
Attendees						
Purpose						
Venue						
				6 Human Needs	My view	Their View
TOPIC		PRESENTER	DURATION	Certainty		
				Uncertainty		
Review of key topics via metrics				Growth		
				Significance		
Department KPI's compared to best in class				Contribution		
				Love		
Personnel						
Leadership development activities						
Action plans for A,B,C players						
Quarterly review of job score card						
Actions from last session						
New actions						
Decion log review						
Confirm next meeting and home work assignments						
Manager take-aways						
Is this leader performing and making progress with their people and their departmental results						
Are there six human needs being met at work						

Spend quality time at work. If you have taken notes and built your plan as you are reading this book, you have set up a series of meetings to set direction, review critical projects, and proactively manage the business, ensuring your team will perform to the financial plan. As a turnaround leader, your team is facing more uncertainty now than ever. Make time for MBWA— "management by walking around." I typically do this daily, mixing up the time in which I walk around the department or building. Sometimes I will do this first thing in the morning, and sometimes it will be the last event of the day. Spend time with people you normally would not interact with, talking and answering questions on the spot. With each walk-around, people will get more comfortable with you. They will eventually start asking the real questions on their minds. This is the moment of truth: If you have an answer, give it then and there with no bias. People are asking to find out if they can trust you. If you do not have an answer, tell them when you will get back to them with an answer, and then ensure that you do. The intention of these walk-around is to show that you care, to be a great listener, and to directly answer questions when asked. Once your team sees that you believe in the company and care about the people, they will be more comfortable with bringing up the real issues and looking to you for leadership.

Leading people during distressed times

Leading people in distressed times within a company takes a portfolio of skills. I have studied this topic for two decades and, while this topic deserves a dedicated book itself, the following summary provides a primer of the fundamentals. Additional information or leadership training can be scheduled at www.robcainconsulting.com.

People won't change unless there is a real, felt need.

Common excuses why people do not listen to advice are

1. I didn't respect/trust the person who was offering the advice.

2. He didn't really understand my situation.

3. She had her own agenda in mind. I had already tried what she suggested.

4. What she suggested really wouldn't work in my situation.

5. The advice was too simplistic; it didn't fully address the underlying issue.

6. I had my own ideas, and I really wanted to try them.

People only decide to change on their own. Your job as the change agent is to have THEM answer the following three questions. (Your answers are meaningless and will actually slow the process of change.)

Can you do it?

Is it worth it to me?

Do I know how to make the shift?

Fundamentals of leading in particularly distressed times

Mutual trust and respect

Set clear direction

Provide the right tools/training

Ensure the six human needs are met

Traits of successful coaching:

My coach genuinely cared about me.

His interest went beyond my immediate job performance.

She challenged me and believed that I was capable of accomplishing more than I thought was possible for myself.

He was candid and straightforward; I knew where I stood with him.

My coach didn't hold grudges; the past stayed in the past.

She listened and understood my point of view.

A trust-based relationship must be in place if coaching is going to work.

Building strong relationships require the following elements:

Desire to connect—The relationship must start with two emotionally healthy people who make a commitment.

Warmth—If relationships were to be categorized along the single dimension of "warm vs. cold," there would be no question that the strongest coaching relationships would be clustered at the "warm" end of the scale.

Flexibility—The same type of relationship that is effective with one direct report will not be as effective with another one.

Creating feedback mechanisms—One of the best ways to make a relationship work is to utilize a variety of methods to increase feedback in both directions.

Use effective leadership practices—The leaders' behavior day after day toward employees obviously makes an enormous impact on the relationship.

Generate trust—Honor commitments, create a safe environment, and do what is right regardless of personal risk or consequences.

Build relationships—Understand and relate well to others.

Avoid Relationship detractors

1. Maintain confidentiality. Coaching conversations will often turn to personal and confidential issues.

2. Be sure to be transparent. Hidden agendas will upset those you are coaching.

3. Be fully present. People can tell when you are really paying attention and when you are there in body only.

4. Keep your commitments.

Example of questions that can be used during a coaching one-on-one meeting

The meeting is the employee's time to hold himself accountable.

The meeting is the manager's time to ensure the six human needs are met while holding the employee accountable.

Use open-ended questions:

"How do you feel about the solution and timing of project XYZ?"

"What are your thoughts about how we can be more innovative than our competitors with our XYZ process?"

"As you know, we lost a deal last week. What are your thoughts on how our team can become stronger as a result of that?"

"Can you share your progress on your development plan? I'm particularly interested in ABC."

CHAPTER 7

Accelerating Top Line Growth at Lower Costs

Chapter deliverables:

1. Defining education-based selling

2. Increasing your close rates and shorten the cycle time to close

3. Establishing a closed-loop selling process and increasing your close rate through education-based selling and not product selling

4. Defining multiple go-to market strategies

5. Being more creative than your competitors

6. Falling in love with your customers

Defining education based selling as provided to us by Chet Holmes

There are three ways to grow the top line of a business: (1) Sell to more customers, (2) increase the amount of the customer transaction, and (3) sell at a higher frequency. The trick is to implement two out of three of these items to profitably grow your top line.

As with any process, it's best to understand the performance data of the process to better visualize the value chain and know where to place your efforts. In one project, our close rate was a miserable 19 percent. We doubled that in four months. Clearly, if you start measuring something that was not measured or held accountable in the past, people wake up and start selling. People also wake up and take notice when you change out the leaders of the Sales team. I am convinced that our results would have been far less impressive without business consultant Chet Holmes and his advice.

Chet described education-based selling as teaching, not selling. With education-based sales, you are teaching the customer about the problems in their space or field and why it's important they solve those problems. Naturally, the products your company sells solve their problems. By taking a teaching approach, the salesperson is no longer focused on pushing a product. The salesperson now has a dialogue with the customer about the industry and how to solve the current and future problems the customer faces.

In one project we held a four-session course with our sales team and the executive team in order to develop education-based selling tools together. We worked through a "stadium pitch" and the scripts, which gave our sales team the confidence to lead a conversation with anyone. Our course covered nine items.

1. The salesperson is established as an expert.

2. The salesperson has scripts and a stadium pitch to keep the audience wanting more.

3. The sales team is smarter.

4. Sales materials gain significant credibility when they begin with market data.

5. The company controls the material covered and can easily unseat its competitors.

6. With education-based selling, you can have a conversation with almost anyone, including the 90 percent of people that are not buying today.

7. It's easier to get to a closing conversation.

8. It's easier to get appointments.

9. It creates brand loyalty.

Education based selling positions the sales team as industry experts

In addition, we also incorporated a weekly follow-up impact meeting to discuss why we won or lost an order that week. As part of this, we only allowed lost orders to fit into one of three categories: Product gap, marketing alignment, or sales skills. Each of these categories had an owner and an action plan in order to resolve the issue and be able to close the sale in the future.

This particular team had gotten comfortable with the routine of having five or six conversations with a potential new customer before a close. In the second week of using the new tools, the sales team began closing deals after one conversation. The shift to education-based selling changed the confidence level in this sales team. The accountability factor of expecting to close an order and following that through in a weekly sales impact meeting was a game changer for this project.

There are three ways to grow a company:
- Acquire more customers
- Increase the transaction amount
- Increase the frequency of transactions

Finally, at the same time we implemented a CRM system, which enabled our sales team to work wherever and whenever they wanted. As a commission-based team, many salespeople went back to work after having dinner and completing familial obligations.

Implement multiple go-to market strategies for your business. Most companies have one main go-to market strategy; when that critical path is impacted, companies' top lines suffer. There are over twenty ways to reach your customers. The trick is to find which ones work for your company and then implement them. Below are ten examples of ways to reach your customers:

1. Outbound sales
2. Inbound sales as a result of advertising campaigns
3. Direct mail
4. Referrals
5. Web-based advertising
6. White labeling
7. Web site
8. Agent programs
9. Retail store partnerships
10. Joint ventures

Study your customers' spending habits and learn how they analyze your offering. Do they investigate it on the web or through referrals? Do they cold call your sales team? Win-loss reports and weekly impact meetings are the right place to dive into this level of detail in order to continually refine your offer, web site, advertising, and go-to market strategies.

Customers purchase products and services to solve their problems. Ensure they will be well taken care of before, during, and after the purchase. Ensure your go-to market solution set clearly differentiates you from your competitors in terms of value and customer care.

CHAPTER 8
Strategic Planning Process

Chapter deliverables:

1. The elements that make up the annual planning process

2. How to deeply engage the team in the business plan

A company becomes distressed because it has elements of a flawed plan and the wrong assumptions to operate the business, and it is not proactive in resolving either of these issues. The strategic planning process is another opportunity for the *new* team to further resolve these issues by exercising their due diligence skills; identifying the current strengths and weaknesses of their company, their competitors, and the market; and building the right plan for the year ahead.

The goals of a strategic planning process are to develop a comprehensive plan for the coming year and to educate the team of this plan. Many teams within distressed companies believe they understand both the market and their competitor's offerings and tend to develop a new financial plan in a vacuum using product and marketing materials not updated from the prior year. The result is the same old story: continually decaying results. In addition, the team continues its inside-out thinking and is not informed or prepared to deal with the problems that will come in the year ahead.

Setting the stage for the annual plan is important. I typically require involvement from several people, from the C-level management team to the first-line manager. Teams are formed for core parts of the business; special teams are also assigned to address issues within the business and in the market. Kickoff meetings, which wake up the team and push them into action, are best held offsite and should include an external keynote speaker. Keynote speakers can be a key customer, a market analyst, or a venture capital investor in the field. Keynote speakers can even be a competitor, if it's appropriate. There is a new day ahead, and it requires a new plan.

Involving the management team makes the team much smarter and owners of the plan moving forward

Breakout teams are formally assigned in the kickoff meeting and given a timeline and a set of deliverables then. Classic breakout teams focus on a very specific topic, which may include financial, marketing, sales, operations, service, products, and people/culture as topics. As time is critical, be emphatic about the quality and format of the deliverables. Typically, each team is required to prepare a financial analysis that rolls up into the financial plan, a set of measureable objectives that include quarterly deliverables, and a PowerPoint document that will be part of the BoD presentation. Depending on your situation, you may choose to bring in outside experts for the steering committee or breakout teams.

Breakout teams will present and debate with the entire team or committee. The intent is to ensure the deliverables are accurate and measurable and produce the right level of results.

In most cases, it's best to start with the results of the marketing breakout team to ensure that the entire team is well aligned to the changes in the market and how to best drive top line. The results of this team are typically precursors for the sales, product, and financial teams.

The following are a few of the tools we typically assign to help the team start its due diligence process.

Core competency review/update

Market update and SWOT

Competitor analysis and SWOT

Company SWOT

Product roadmap (included IP)

People related information update: Compensation, reward programs, performance evaluations.

The following graphic is a typical process for a strategic planning process, as well as the synchronization of the breakout teams.

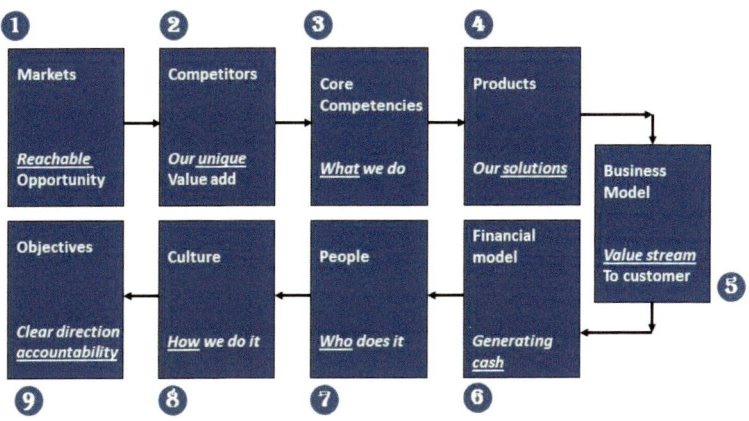

Presenting to the BoD is another level of getting the team involved and taking ownership in the business. Presenting the breakout teams' findings and how they plan to grow and improve the business is another small part of instilling a culture of accountability and execution.

About the Author

Rob has 25 years' experience in improving the performance of companies. Results for distressed companies that fully implement the smart business system methodology can yield 50-200% YOY EBITDA improvement within 12–18 months.

Rob earned an Engineering degree and an MBA before beginning his career in the capital equipment space developing new products for the commercial aerospace markets and finding unique ways to improve product performance while lowering cost. Later, Rob help lead the growth and renovation initiatives of an OEM capital equipment company in the rail space taking the company public in 1995.

Further in his career, as the newly assigned president of a European division capital equipment company, Rob found himself crossing picket lines within the division he was recently assigned. Needing to ship the products that were on the floor to make payroll, Rob crossed the picket lines, assembled a company meeting, and described the facts of the business and how the team could continue to exist and become profitable by working together with a focused vision. In the coming months, the failing division was transformed into a Sales/Service office that yielded positive cash flow.

Rob was later trained in Six Sigma practices and how to lead people within companies in distressed times, further learning how to inspire teams to new levels of performance through trust, focus, accountability, and the six human needs.

As an officer and BoD Member of a global capital equipment company, the leadership team increased EBITDA three times in three years, instilling a culture of accountability and execution in a unionized environment while finding ways to outperform competitors worldwide. As a C-level manager in a SaaS company, the team posted 200%+ YOY EBITDA growth in 18 months.

Today, Rob coaches leadership teams and CEOs on how to improve the performance of their companies by instilling a cash-driven culture of accountability and execution along with the focus, process and leadership skills required to inspire teams and senior leaders to new levels of performance.

CPSIA information can be obtained
at www.ICGtesting.com
Printed in the USA
LVIC072231020713
341304LV00001B